FIRSTHAND SUCCESS

ENGLISH FIRSTHAND BEGINNERS' COURSE

Marc Helgesen
Steven Brown
Ruth Venning

Development editor
Michael Rost

Consulting editor
Minoru Wada
Japanese Ministry of Education

LINGUAL HOUSE

Firsthand SUCCESS

Marc Helgesen, Steven Brown, and Ruth Venning

ISBN	textbook	0 582 07969 1
	workbook	0 582 07971 3
	cassettes	0 582 07959 4
	manual	0 582 07970 5

This book was developed for Longman Group by Lateral Communications Ltd.

Fourth impression 1992

Printed in Hong Kong
SC/04

development editor: Michael Rost
project coordinator: Keiko Kimura
text design: Kato Kotaro Design Studio
cover design: Kotaro Kato
recording supervisor: Masahiro Someya

photograph credits: Hiroyuki Shinohara, Ken Kitamura, Orion Press, Mon-Tresor, American Photo Library, Kyodo News Service, Mainichi Shinbunsha, Keiko Kimura

illustration credits: Tadashi Hirota, Misa Nishimura, Shack Mihara, Suzy Yamaoka, Mamoru Ikeuchi

recording credits: Michael Worman, Johua Popenoe, Paul Silverman, Maya Sackheim, Franca Cataldo, Deborah Kathrine, Mary Ann Decker, Hank Roberts, Lyn Harris, Irene Olshewsky, Charles Sandy, Bill Bickard, Larry Frumson, Denise Moore, Terry Osada, Rumiko Varnes, George Reseter

Dedication:
This book is dedicated to high school teachers, who often don't get credit for the devoted job they are doing, to our students, who made the project worthwhile, and to our families, especially to Masumi and Kent, for everything they've done to support us.

Acknowledgements:
We would like to thank the following people for reviewing and piloting earlier versions of this textbook and for giving us useful feedback:

Carolyn Adams, Doreen Blas, Margaret Chang, Dale Griffee, Andrew House, Kathryn Hill, Masumi Hori, Kayo Hosomi, Gwen Joy, Hiroshi Kano, Kenji Koshida, Yoshie Miyahara, Hajime Otake, Laurie Peters, Kay Reed, Carol Sasaki, Joanne Sauber, Peppy Scott, Masaru Seto, Sharon Setoguchi, Dorolyn Smith, Daniel Talbot, Hiroshi Tanaka, Joseph Tomei, Setsuko Toyama, Munetsugu Uruno, Seiichi Yoshida, Lori Zenuk-Nishide. And special thanks to Minoru Wada for his guidance and support of this project.

We would also like to thank the staff of Longman ELT for their support of this and other Lingual House projects. In particular, thanks to: Tim Hunt, Damien Tunnacliffe, Louise Elkins, Shinsuke Suzuki, Hiromi Tsuchiya, Kevin Bergman, Takashi Hata, Yoko Hibi, Hideki Komiyama, Yoko Honjo, and Erika Miyoshi.

Finally, we would like to thank our editor, Michael Rost, our project coordinator, Keiko Kimura, and our chief text designer, Kotaro Kato for their direction, insights, and encouragement. M.H. S.B. R.V.

Introduction

Firsthand SUCCESS helps students learn English by actually using the language to communicate, rather than simply practicing language patterns and fixed conversations. Like *Firsthand ACCESS,* the first book in this series, *Firsthand SUCCESS* is intended for students who have had little or no experience with spoken English.

Firsthand SUCCESS is designed for use in a variety of settings. Because the course incorporates extensive use of pair practice, *Firsthand SUCCESS* is suitable for large classes in which the teacher has limited one-to-one contact with individual students. The pair practice in *Firsthand SUCCESS* provides students with clear and meaningful outcomes so that the students can perform and check much of their classroom work without direct teacher assistance.

In order to promote actual *communicative use* of the new language (and not merely simulated conversations), *Firsthand SUCCESS* provides learners with interesting and exciting activities that draw upon the students' own experience, imagination and ideas. In this way, *SUCCESS* deals with the common problems (particularly in many EFL—English as a Foreign Language—settings) of students who are not highly motivated to participate in classes where active use of the new language is encouraged.

Firsthand SUCCESS features an integrated syllabus that has an easily recognizable progression of grammar, functions, vocabulary and pronunciation points, as well as a graded sequence of tasks. The base syllabus in *SUCCESS* is English sentence structure. Sentence structures are presented in relation to everyday functions and are expanded to include natural sequences of conversation. Additionally, a graded *speechwork* (pronunciation) section allows the students to practice various intonation and stress patterns which are so important in effective use of English. Finally, essential vocabulary and language clarification routines are introduced and recycled in activities throughout the course.

Each unit of *Firsthand SUCCESS* consists of six parts: *conversation, listening, speechwork, pair work, reading for meaning* and *review*. The *Firsthand SUCCESS* CASSETTES, which are essential for the effective use of the course, contain the *conversations,* the segments for the *listening* sections, models for the *speechwork* (pronunciation) sections and recorded versions of *reading for meaning*. A **WORKBOOK** for additional practice is available separately. A detailed **TEACHER'S MANUAL**, also available separately, includes *lesson plans (with specific ideas for team-teaching), language & culture notes, expansion activities, classroom management techniques* and *quizzes*.

CONVERSATION

The *Conversation* page features a four-part picture sequence which illustrates the language points of the unit in a familiar context. The *Conversations* all allow for substitution, so that the students can learn dialogs without word-for-word memorization. In this way, the students, even at the beginning of their study of English, are encouraged to make original choices (and listen for their partner's original choices), while maintaining reasonable accuracy. One *Conversation* model for each unit is on the cassette tape.

LISTENING

All listening activities are to be used with the recorded material on the *Firsthand SUCCESS* cassettes. The warming up activities are introductory exercises which give listening practice and, at the same time, present important vocabulary to be used later in the unit. The main listening activities involve the students in listening for *selected information*. In order to keep the students focused on listening, the activities in this section entail a minimum of reading and writing. Because the activities can be checked quickly, the teacher can receive feedback about what the students do and do not understand.

SPEECHWORK

Speechwork activities, located near the end of the book, are done after the main listening activity. The first part of each *Speechwork*, which is included on the tape, provides examples of correct pronunciation and intonation. This introduction is followed by a *Speechwork* activity to be practiced in pairs.

PAIR WORK

The central activity of each unit is an information-gap *Pair work* exercise. In this pair work activity, students do more than mimic conversations. They use English to exchange information. Language patterns that are needed in the activity are highlighted in order to allow for preparatory practice and to serve as a ready reference during the task itself. The tasks make extensive use of ideas and opinions.

Each *Pair work* begins with a quick practice of the language in the reference table at the top of the page. Through examples provided in this reference box, the teacher can highlight the upcoming situation and exemplify the procedures needed for the pair work task. After this preparation, the class is divided in pairs (usually students sitting across from each other assume "A" and "B" roles). Each pair engages in the task while the teacher circulates, providing help with procedure and corrections of major language problems.

A separate follow-up task, called *Challenge!* is provided at the bottom of each *Pair work* page to ensure that students who finish the main task early can continue to engage in useful and interesting practice.

READING FOR MEANING

The *Reading for meaning* section in each unit presents an interesting reading passage tied to the theme of the unit. In line with the communicative methodology that *SUCCESS* employs, each passage is designed to be read as a whole unit, with students focusing on understanding the gist of the text, rather than stopping to study language forms in it.

Although most students in EFL classes can read at a higher level of proficiency than they can speak, many have never experienced reading English *for meaning*—that is, focusing on the content of the text without being required to translate sentences or note down unfamiliar vocabulary words. To help students understand the meaning as well as develop concrete reading skills, preview questions are provided at the top of the page. These allow students to identify the topic and to know what they are trying to learn from the reading. Consistent with principles of language development, the readings in *SUCCESS* employ a level of syntax and vocabulary that is more advanced than the language used for production in other sections of the unit.

REVIEW

The *Review* page of each unit provides a vocabulary exercise as well as an open conversation, *Talking to Vince*, which helps the students to consolidate their learning. Additionally, in most units, the *Review* page offers *Check it out!*—easy to understand explanations or reminders of sometimes troublesome language points.

In using this course, your students do more than practice and parrot scripted examples of English. They actually use English to communicate. They experience ***Firsthand SUCCESS***.

FIRSTHAND
SUCCESS

ENGLISH FIRSTHAND BEGINNERS' COURSE

CONTENTS

Where are you going?

 Step 1: Listen.
Step 2: Practice.

go ahead
have a seat

Montreal
Seattle

Montreal
Seattle

how interesting
that's interesting

Getting to know you.

Step 1: Write these words:

who what when where how do

What 's your name?

_____ do you get to school?

_____ do you get up?

_____ is your favorite sport?

_____ is your favorite musician?

_____ do you do in your free time?

_____ you like English?

**Step 2: Listen to the interview.
Write the answers.**

How do you spell that?

1. Name: _Brian_ _____

2. Address: _____

3. Gets to school: _____

4. Gets up: _____

5. Goes to bed: _____

6. Favorite food: _____

7. Favorite musician: _____

8. Free time activity: _____

9. Favorite sport: _____

10. Like English? _____

About you.   **Answer the questions.**

1. _____
2. _____
3. _____
4. _____
5. _____
6. _____
7. _____

Now try Speechwork 1. **A,** look at page 73. **B,** look at page 74.

My Partner

How do you spell it?

You will interview your partner.

**Step 1: Ask B the questions.
Write B's answers.**

What does favorite mean?

It means the one you like most.

1. Name: _____
   What's your name?

2. Address: _____
   Where do you live?

3. Gets to school: _____
   How do you get to school?

4. Gets up: _____
   When do you get up?

5. Goes to bed: _____
   When do you go to bed?

6. Favorite food: _____
   What is your favorite food?

7. Favorite sport: _____
   What is your favorite sport?

8. Favorite musician: _____
   Who is your favorite musician?

9. Free time activity: _____
   What do you do in your free time?

10. Likes English?: _____
    Do you like English?

**Step 2: Work in groups of 4.
Introduce B.**

This is Naomi.		
She He	comes to school	by bus. on foot.
	gets up goes to bed	at 6 o'clock. at 11:30 (eleven-thirty).
	likes doesn't like	pizza. Michael Jackson. baseball. English.
Her favorite His favorite	sport food	is tennis. is ice cream.

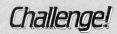

Close your book.
Can you remember three things about each person?

My Partner

How do you spell it?

You will interview your partner.

**Step 1: Ask A the questions.
Write A's answers.**

What does <u>favorite</u> mean?

It means <u>the</u> one you like most.

1. Name: _____
   What's your name?

2. Address: _____
   Where do you live?

3. Gets to school: _____
   How do you get to school?

4. Gets up: _____
   When do you get up?

5. Goes to bed: _____
   When do you go to bed?

6. Favorite food: _____
   What is your favorite food?

7. Favorite sport: _____
   What is your favorite sport?

8. Favorite musician: _____
   Who is your favorite musician?

9. Free time activity: _____
   What do you do in your free time?

10. Likes English?: _____
    Do you like English?

**Step 2: Work in groups of 4.
Introduce A.**

This is Naomi.		
She He	comes to school	by bus. on foot.
	gets up goes to bed	at 6 o'clock. at 11:30 (eleven-thirty).
	likes doesn't like	pizza. Michael Jackson. baseball. English.
Her favorite His favorite	sport food	is tennis. is ice cream.

Challenge!   Close your book.
Can you remember three things about each person?

First names

What names are popular in your country?
Write three.

_____
_____
_____

Why were you given your name?

Read and answer
- Why do names become popular?

  _____
  _____
  _____

- Find an unusual name in the story.

  _____

Parents decide on their children's names for many reasons. Some parents give their child the same name as a grandparent, aunt or uncle. Others use the name of a famous person in the news or a popular movie star. Sometimes parents give names just because they like the sound.

ASK THE PEOPLE
How did you choose your child's name?

June Palmer,
homemaker

My baby's name is Steven but we call him Stevie. We like Stevie Wonder a lot. We didn't really name our baby after Stevie Wonder, but I think he made us notice the name.

Stevie Wonder is such a great musician. Even though he's a superstar, he still tries to help other people who aren't so lucky.

One more thing—when my husband and I met, Stevie Wonder's song *I Just Called* was really popular.

Aug. 18

Dear Aunt Elizabeth,

It's a girl! Our baby was born last Thursday. She is <u>so</u> beautiful. Jenny is still in the hospital but she is OK. They'll come home next week.

We thought you would be happy to hear that we named her after you— Elizabeth Ann.

You've always been Jenny's favorite aunt and we hope our little Elizabeth grows up to be just like you.

I'll write again soon.

Love,

Paul

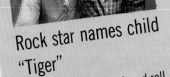

Rock star names child "Tiger"

(San Francisco) Rock and roll musician J.J. James and his wife, Patti, became parents today. James announced that they named the baby boy "Tiger." When asked why they selected such an unusual name, James said, "We wanted an unusual name and we really like tigers. They are strong and colorful. The animals are unique. They are not like any other animal. My son will be unique, too. He doesn't need to be like everyone else. He'll be his own person."

The words are mixed up.
Write the questions.
Answer them.

Questions:

Answers:

• your   what's   name

What's your name?

My name's

• sport   is   your   favorite   what

_____ ?

_____

• live   where   you   do

_____ ?

_____

• get   to   how   school   do   you

_____ ?

_____

• you   up   when   do   get

_____ ?

_____

• time   your   you   do   do   what   in   free

_____ ?

_____

• English   you   like   do

_____ ?

_____

Vince: Hi! I'm Vince.

You: *I'm* _____

Vince: Where do you live?

You: _____

Vince: What is your favorite food?

You: _____

Vince: I like that, too.
Who is your favorite musician?

You: _____

Vince: Really?
What do you do in your free time?

You: _____

What   ?

Vince: In my free time? I sleep.

Let's get a pet.

 Step 1: Listen.
Step 2: Practice.

Let's get a <u>cat</u>.

I don't know.
They are <u>a lot of</u> trouble.

| dog | too much |
| bird | so much |

Well, they're <u>cleaner</u> than <u>birds</u>.

Maybe, but they aren't as <u>clean</u> as fish.

| better | cats | good |
| easier | dogs | easy |

Come on!
<u>Cats</u> are <u>more interesting</u> than <u>fish</u>.

Maybe.

| dogs | more beautiful | cats |
| birds | less expensive | dogs |

What kind of pet do you want?

A what?

I know!
Let's get a <u>monkey</u>!

frog
turtle

Your nature IQ

How much do you know about nature?

Step 1: Read the questions. What do you think? Check (✓) your answers.

1. Which grows the **fastest**? ☐ a sunflower ☑ bamboo ☐ a pineapple

2. Which is the **most intelligent**? ☐ a pig ☐ a monkey ☐ a dog

3. Which can live **longer** without drinking water? ☐ a camel ☐ a giraffe

4. Which is **noisier**? ☐ a mouse ☐ a giraffe

5. Which is **bigger**? ☐ The Atlantic Ocean ☐ The Pacific Ocean

6. Where is the **highest** waterfall?
   ☐ Africa
   ☐ North America
   ☐ South America

7. Where is the **tallest** tree?
   ☐ Australia
   ☐ Africa
   ☐ North America

8. Which has the **most islands**?
   ☐ Canada
   ☐ Indonesia
   ☐ Japan

9. Which is **more dangerous** to people? ☐ a gorilla ☐ a crocodile

10. Are there **more kinds** of ☐ cats or ☐ bats?

Step 2: Listen. Circle the answers.

How many did you guess correctly? _____

Now try Speechwork 2. **A,** look at page 73. **B,** look at page 74.

Animal ESP

....

	That's right.	
Is it a dog?	No,	it's fast**er than** a dog. it's **more** dangerous **than** a dog. it's **less** friendly **than** a dog. but it's **as** smart **as** a dog. it's not **as** popular **as** a dog.

What does ___ mean?

Do you believe in telepathy? This is an ESP test.
You will compare some animals. Can you send messages just by thinking?

Think of an animal. B will guess.
If B is wrong, answer by comparing. Use these words:

Short words: add **er**	Two syllable words that end in **y**: change **y** to **i**, add **er**	Long words: use **more**

fast**er**/slow**er**
loud**er**
big**ger**/small**er**/larg**er**
tall**er**/short**er**/long**er**
light**er**
cut**er**
smart**er**

friendl**ier**
prett**ier**/ugl**ier**
sill**ier**
funn**ier** looking
heav**ier**
nois**ier**

more beautiful
more dangerous
more intelligent
more interesting
more popular

Play 6 times.
Count your guesses:

1.	
2.	
3.	
4.	
5.	
6.	

horse
insect
monkey
gorilla
dog
cow
fox
bat
mouse
kangaroo
elephant
bear
giraffe
rabbit
hippo
snake
camel
bird
koala
tiger
crocodile
turtle
cat
lion
pig

Add the total guesses. _____
Divide (÷) by 6.
What is your average? _____

In your class, who had the lowest average? _____
They have the best ESP.

Challenge!   Close your book.
Think of teachers in your school. **B** will guess.

PAIR WORK **B**

Animal ESP

....

Is it a dog?	That's right.	
	No,	it's fast**er than** a dog. it's **more** dangerous **than** a dog. it's **less** friendly **than** a dog. but it's **as** smart **as** a dog. it's not **as** popular **as** a dog.

What does _____ mean?

Do you believe in telepathy? This is an ESP test.
You will compare some animals. Can you send messages just by thinking?

Think of an animal. A will guess.
If A is wrong, answer by comparing. Use these words:

Short words: add **er**	Two syllable words that end in **y**: change **y** to **i**, add **er**	Long words: use **more**

fast**er**/slow**er**
loud**er**
big**ger**/small**er**/larg**er**
tall**er**/short**er**/long**er**
light**er**
cut**er**
smart**er**

friend**lier**
prett**ier**/ug**lier**
sill**ier**
funn**ier** looking
heav**ier**
nois**ier**

more beautiful
more dangerous
more intelligent
more interesting
more popular

Play 6 times.
Count your guesses:

1.
2.
3.
4.
5.
6.

horse
insect
monkey
gorilla
dog
cow
fox
bat
mouse
kangaroo
elephant
bear
giraffe
rabbit
hippo
tiger
snake
camel
bird
koala
crocodile
turtle
cat
lion
pig

Add the total guesses. _____
Divide (÷) by 6.
What is your average? _____

In your class, who had the lowest average? _____
They have the best ESP.

Challenge!	Close your book. Think of teachers in your school. **A** will guess.

Are people like animals?

In your language do you compare people to animals?
What expressions do you use?

Read and answer

• When do children "play possum?"

_____

_____

• What does it mean to call someone "a turkey?"

_____

This is an opossum. It is one of the most unusual animals in America.
The opossum is a member of the same animal family as the kangaroo:
marsupial. Marsupial mothers carry their babies in a pocket called
a pouch. Opossums live in North and South America. They are the only
pouched animal that does not live in Australia.

When opossums are chased by dogs or other animals, they fall down
and lie still. They act like they are dead. The dog is usually so surprised
that it walks away without hurting the opossum. Then the opossum runs
away. Pretending that you are sick or hurt is called "playing possum."
If children do not want to go to school, they sometimes
tell their mothers that they are sick.
They are "playing possum."

Have you ever "played possum?"

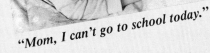

"Mom, I can't go to school today."

This is a turkey. It is one of the largest birds in the world. Most weigh about
12 kilograms, but some of the biggest turkeys weigh over 35 kg. Turkeys,
which cannot fly, came from North America but can now be found in
Europe, too. Their name is a mistake. The people who named them thought
they were the same as birds from the country of Turkey.

Turkeys are one of the least intelligent animals. Sometimes when it rains,
turkeys look at the sky. They forget to put their heads back down.

Because the birds are so stupid, people sometimes use the word "turkey"
to mean a "silly" or "foolish" person. For example, if your friend does
something silly or foolish, you might say, "You turkey!"

Has anyone ever called <u>you</u> a "turkey?"

"You did what?"

Do these adjectives use **er** or **more**?
Finish the sentences.

• A cat is   **pretty**/ *ier*   than a _COW._

• A monkey ∧ *more* **intelligent**   than a _____ .

• English is   **interesting**   than _____ .

• A koala is   **cute**   than a _____ .

• A(n) _____ is   **popular**   than a rabbit.

• A bicycle is   **expensive**   than a _____ .

• A(n) _____ is   **ugly**   than a turtle.

• A dog is   **silly**   than a _____ .

• My city is   **big**   than _____ .

• A(n) _____ is   **dangerous**   than a fox.

• A car is   **noisy**   than a _____ .

Check it out!

> ✔ Use -**er**/-**est** with short (one-syllable) adjectives and -**ier**/-**iest** with adjectives that end with **y**.
> •   ••
> [big→bigger, pretty→prettier]
>
> ✔ Use **more**/**most** with long adjectives.

Talking to Vince

Vince: What's your favorite animal?

You: _____ .

Vince: Why?

You: _They're   er_ .

Vince: That's true. Any other reason?

You: _They're more_ .

Vince: Yes.

You: _And they're not as_

_____ .

Vince: I guess you're right.

You: _What_   ?

Vince: My favorite?
I like flamingos!

How about a movie?

Step 1: Listen.
Step 2: Practice.

Let's go somewhere today.

OK. A movie?

this afternoon
tomorrow

Yeah.
Let's go to *The Dark Secret*.

Well, I like love stories better than horror movies.

Jungle Adventure
Star X

adventure
science fiction

How about *Gone with the Wind?*

Hmm. I really prefer new movies.

modern
more recent

Anything is OK.
I just want to be with you.

You do?

all right
fine

oh
really

I like the country.

Step 1: Which do you prefer? **Check (✓) your answer.**

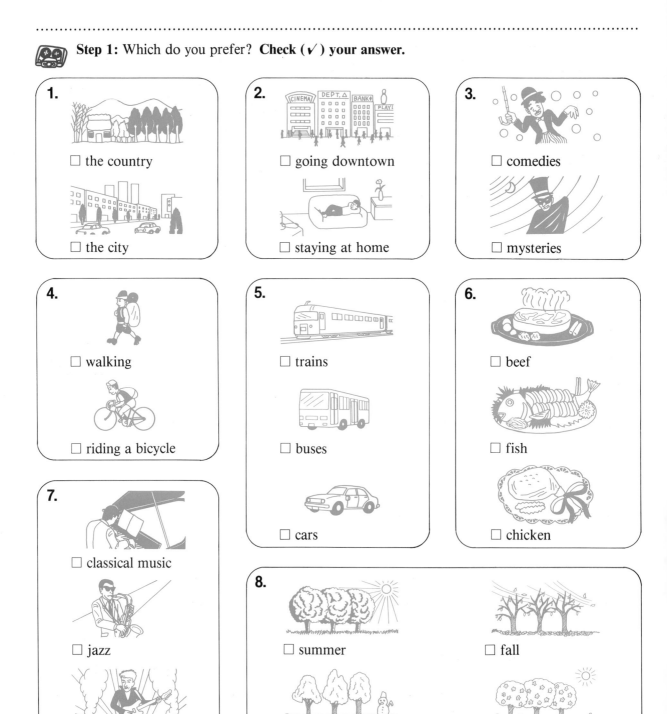

1.
☐ the country
☐ the city

2.
☐ going downtown
☐ staying at home

3.
☐ comedies
☐ mysteries

4.
☐ walking
☐ riding a bicycle

5.
☐ trains
☐ buses
☐ cars

6.
☐ beef
☐ fish
☐ chicken

7.
☐ classical music
☐ jazz
☐ rock

8.
☐ summer
☐ fall
☐ winter
☐ spring

Step 2: Listen. Circle the thing each speaker likes.

Now try Speechwork 3. **A,** look at page 75. **B,** look at page 76.

Which do you like better?

Which do you	**prefer, like better,**	rock or jazz?	I	like rock better. prefer jazz.
Which do you	**like best, prefer,**	rock, jazz or classical music?	I	prefer rock like jazz (the) best.

Step 1: Check (✓) the one you think B likes better.

☐ classical music 　or ☐ jazz

☐ the ocean 　or ☐ the mountains

☐ fall **or** ☐ summer

☐ the country **or** ☐ big cities

☐ being busy 　**or** ☐ having nothing to do

☐ going downtown **or** ☐ staying at home

☐ comedies 　☐ mysteries 　**or** ☐ love stories

☐ dogs 　☐ cats 　**or** ☐ birds

☐ _____ **or** ☐ _____
(Write the names of two movies)

☐ _____ ☐ _____ **or** ☐ _____
(Write the names of three sports)

Excuse me?

How do you say _____ in English?

Step 2: Ask B. Circle B's answers.

How many did you guess correctly? _____

0-4 = You don't know B very well. 5-7 = You know B well. 8-10 = You really know what B likes!

 Close your book. What does **B** like that you don't?
Find 5 things. Write your answers.

PAIR WORK **B**

Which do you like better?

....

Which do you	**prefer,** **like better,**	rock or jazz?	I	like rock better. prefer jazz.
Which do you	**like best,** **prefer,**	rock, jazz or classical music?	I	prefer rock like jazz (the) best.

Step 1: Check (✓) the one you think A likes better.

☐ fall ___ **or** ☐ spring ___

☐ cities **or** ☐ small towns

☐ plays **or** ☐ movies

Excuse me?

☐ Sunday **or** ☐ Saturday

☐ walking ___ **or** ☐ riding a bicycle ___

How do you say _____ in English?

☐ reading magazines **or** ☐ reading books

☐ beef ___ ☐ chicken ___ **or** ☐ fish ___

☐ traveling by train ___ ☐ traveling by bus ___ **or** ☐ traveling by car ___

☐ _____ **or** ☐ _____
(Write the names of two cities)

☐ _____ ☐ _____ **or** ☐ _____
(Write the names of three kinds of food)

Step 2: Ask A. Circle A's answers.

How many did you guess correctly? _____

0-4 = You don't know A very well. 5-7 = You know A well. 8-10 = You really know what A likes!

 **Challenge!**   Close your book. What does **A** like that you don't?
Find 5 things. Write your answers.

Americans and TV

What kinds of TV shows are popular in your country?
Which do you like best?

Read and answer

- Find the word "prime time."
  What does it mean?

  _____

- What days do the fewest people watch prime
  time TV?

  _____

  Why do you think fewer people watch on
  those days?

  _____

  _____

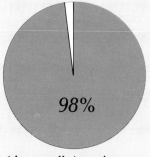

Almost all American
homes have at least one
television set. Many
have more than one.

One out of every three
people thinks that
watching TV is the best
way to spend an evening.

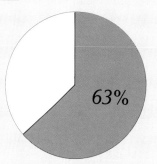

About two-thirds of
American teenagers
watch TV almost
every night.

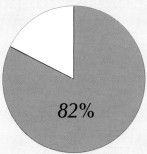

Most adults watch TV shows
between 8 and 11 p.m. This is
called "prime time." That's
when the most popular shows
are broadcast.

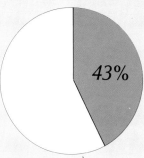

Less than half watch
daytime programs
nearly every day.
Most are game shows
or continuing dramas
called "soap operas."

When we watch TV

Sunday and Monday are the
most popular days for prime
time TV. Family shows and
sports are shown on those
nights. The fewest people watch
on Friday and Saturday evenings.

Write the words.

Across →

1.
2.
3.
4.
5.
6.

Down ↓

7.
8.
9.
10.
11.
12.

Check it out!

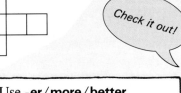

✔ Use **-er** / **more** / **better**
   if you have 2 choices
   [rock or jazz]

✔ Use **-est** / **most** / **best**
   If you have 3 or more choices
   [rock, jazz or classical].

Talking to Vince

Vince: What kind of movies do you like?

You: _____

Vince: Really? Which do you prefer,
new movies or classics?

You: _____

Vince: How about movie stars?
Who's your favorite star?

You: _____

Vince: My favorite movie star? Me, of course.
Do you want to see my home movies?

You: _____

I can't wait!

 Step 1: Listen.
Step 2: Practice.

winter
spring

skiing   go to my grandparents' house
hiking   have a part-time job

have a great time
hate to come back to school

art   work on
music   do

What are you going to do?

....

Step 1: Listen. Write: am going to   am not going to   will   won't
Will you do these things?
Circle **YES** or **NO**.

1. I _am going to_ go shopping this weekend.   Yes   No

2. I probably _____ visit my relatives this summer.   Yes   No

3. I think I _____ get a new pet soon.   Yes   No

4. I _____ probably rent a video this month.   Yes   No

5. I _____ go running this evening.   Yes   No

6. I _____ to learn to type someday.   Yes   No

Step 2: Listen. What are they talking about? Number the pictures.

read about
space travel

play tennis and volleyball,
ride a bicycle

learn to
type

go skiing

get married

graduate

1 study

go to the hospital

Now try Speechwork 4. **A,** look at page 75. **B,** look at page 76.

What are you going to do this weekend?

Is Are	she you they	**going to**	play soccer visit the USA	this Sunday? next summer? soon?	Yes, that's right. Not exactly. No, they aren't
Will	you he	be a teacher graduate	in ten years? next year?	No, I won't.

I don't know.

What are they going to do? **You will guess 1, 3, 5, and 7. B will guess 2, 4, 6, and 8.**
Example: Is he going to read a book tonight?   No, he isn't.
              Is he going to watch TV tonight?   That's right.

B's picture

 guesses

He's going to watch
TV tonight.

1. She's going to _____
   _____ this Sunday.

 B's guesses

2. He's going to ride
   his bicycle tomorrow.

I don't understand.

3. He's going to _____
   _____ next weekend.

 B's guesses

4. She'll ski this winter.

 B's guesses

5. He'll learn _____
   _____ this summer.

 B's guesses

6. They'll get married in
   a few years.

7. She'll _____
   in two years.

 B's guesses

8. She's going to
   study tonight.

Your guesses: _____   B's guesses: _____

Challenge!   What will you do next weekend? Next year? In five years?
Give hints. **B** will guess.

What are you going to do this weekend?

Is Are	she you they	**going to**	play soccer visit the USA	this Sunday? next summer? soon?	Yes, that's right. Not exactly. No, they aren't
Will	you he	be a teacher graduate		in ten years? next year?	No, I won't.

I don't know

What are they going to do? **You will guess 2, 4, 6, and 8. A will guess 1, 3, 5, and 7.**
Example: Is he going to read a book tonight?   No, he isn't.
            Is he going to watch TV tonight?   That's right.

A's picture

②
guesses

He's going to watch
TV tonight.

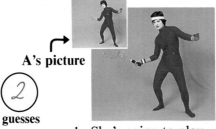

**A's
guesses**

1. She's going to play
    tennis this Sunday.

2. He's going to _____
    ____ _____ tomorrow.

**A's
guesses**

3. He's going to play
    volleyball next weekend.

4. She'll _____
    this winter.

**A's
guesses**

5. He'll learn to type
    this summer.

*I don't
understand.*

6. They'll ____ _____
    in a few years.

**A's
guesses**

7. She'll graduate in
    two years.

8. She's going to
    _____ tonight.

Your guesses: _____   A's guesses: _____

Challenge!

What will you do next weekend? Next year? In five years?
Give hints. **A** will guess.

Knowing the future

How do people in your country try to find out about the future?
Do you think people can know the future?

Read and answer
- What do people ask fortune tellers about?

_____
_____
_____

- What things do fortune tellers use?

_____
_____
_____

   People always want to know about their future. They want to know who they will marry, if they are going to be rich and how long they will live. In many countries, people go to fortune tellers. Fortune tellers are people who say they can "see into the future." Fortune tellers work in different ways. Some use cards. Others use coins. Some even use computers.

   Many fortune tellers look at the lines of a person's hand. They think they can tell if a person will be rich or will marry soon by looking at the lines. This is called palm reading.

   Other fortune tellers use tea leaves. A person drinks the tea and the fortune teller looks at the leaves in the cup. He looks at where the leaves are and the shapes they make. Fortune tellers think that the leaves at the top of the cup show things that are going to happen soon. The leaves at the bottom show what will happen later.

   Many people use the stars to tell the future. They think the place of the stars on someone's birthday can show what kind of life that person will have. This is called "astrology." People can read about astrology every day in most newspapers.

   Even though everyone wants to know about the future, most people don't really believe in fortune tellers. But it is interesting to imagine what will happen.

Write the words.

- holiday = *vacation*

- not right = _____

- finish school = _____

- complete = _____

- tonight = this_____

- mom and dad's parents = _____

- next month, next year = _____

- the day after today = _____

- Saturday and Sunday = _____

- find how to do something = _____

- aunts, uncles, cousins = _____

Find the words.

G	V	E	I	G	N	V	L	A	I	F	N
I	G	N	I	N	E	V	E	T	F	I	N
R	V	A	O	V	A	C	A	T	I	O	N
G	R	A	N	D	P	A	R	E	N	T	S
G	W	W	E	E	K	E	N	D	I	O	D
L	R	E	L	A	T	I	V	E	S	M	V
N	O	A	V	T	A	T	V	S	H	O	R
O	N	W	D	E	T	A	C	V	A	R	O
A	G	X	N	U	N	G	L	Z	B	R	W
P	W	B	N	Q	A	I	X	C	G	O	M
R	R	O	D	F	U	T	U	R	E	W	O
O	N	G	R	E	L	T	E	V	S	E	S

✓ Use **going to** when you are sure something will happen.

✓ Use **will**
   - if you are less certain (OR)
   - at the time you decide.

Check it out!

Talking to Vince

Vince: What are you going to do this weekend?

You: _____

Vince: And after that?

You: _____

Vince: Will you see your friends?

You: _____

Vince: What else will you do?

You: _____

Vince: Anything else?

You: _____

What _____ ?

Vince: Me? I'm going to sleep all weekend. Good night.

What's this?

Step 1: Listen.
Step 2: Practice.

breakfast
dinner

chop vegetables
slice eggs

cook vegetables   wash them
broil fish   fry them

know how to use   to McDonald's
like   out for pizza

What's that for?

Step 1: What are these things used for?
      Write your guesses:

It is used...

- to keep something warm.
- to exercise.
- to carry things.
- to fix a car.
- to bake cookies.
- to teach children.
- to make candy.
- to cook vegetables.

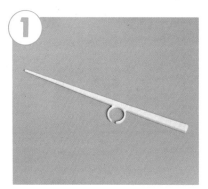

Your guess:
It is used to _____
- She uses it to _____

Your guess:
It is used to _____
- She has it to _____

Your guess:
It is used to _____
- His brother has it to _____

Your guess:
It is used to _____
- He uses it to _____

Your guess:
They are used to _____
- She needs them to _____

Step 2: Listen.
      What are the things for?
      Write the words.

Now try Speechwork 5. **A,** look at page 77. **B,** look at page 78.

I use it to...

What are these things?
B will give you hints.
Count your guesses.

I	use have want need	it them	**to** do my homework. **to** draw. **to** write a letter. **to** write my name.	Is it	a light? an eraser? a typewriter? a pen?

Example:
☐ I use it to do my homework.
☐ I have it to draw.
☐ I need it to write a letter.

Guesses:
• Is it a light?
• Is it an eraser?
• Is it a pen?

I don't know.

It's a pen.

1. use/do my homework
2. have/draw
3. need/write a letter

1. It's a _____

Your guesses: 1 2 3

2. **It's a frying pan.**

B's picture ↓

1. use/cook
2. need/make pancakes
3. want/fry eggs

How do you say _____ in English?

3. These are _____

Your guesses: 1 2 3

4. **It's a muffler** (or **scarf**).

1. use/go outside
2. need/stay warm in winter
3. want/put around my neck

5. It's a _____

Your guesses: 1 2 3

6. **They are pieces of chalk.**

1. use/write
2. need/draw
3. have/write on a chalkboard

7. It's a _____

Your guesses: 1 2 3

8. **It's a helmet.**

1. have it/stay safe
2. use/guard (protect) my head
3. need/ride a motorcycle

Your guesses: _____   **B**'s guesses: _____

 Take five things from your bag or desk. Imagine. What else
could they be? (Example: a pencil could be a microphone
or a rocket.) Give hints. **B** will guess.

I use it to...

What are these things?
A will give you hints.
Count your guesses.

| I | use have want need | it them | **to** do my homework. **to** draw. **to** write a letter. **to** write my name. | Is it | a light? an eraser? a typewriter? a pen? |

Example:
☐ I use it to do my homework.
☐ I have it to draw.
☐ I need it to write a letter.

Guesses:
• Is it a light?
• Is it an eraser?
• Is it a pen?

I don't know.

It's a pen.

1. use/do my homework
2. have/draw
3. need/write a letter

1. **It's an iron.**

 A's picture ↓

1. need/look nice
2. want/take care of clothes
3. have/iron clothes

2. It's a _____

Your guesses: 1 2 3

3. **They are nails.**

1. want/build something
2. use/make a desk
3. need/connect two pieces of wood

4. It's a _____

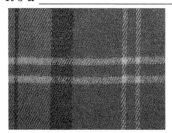

Your guesses: 1 2 3

5. **It's a cushion**

1. have/relax
2. use/rest
3. want/sit on

How do you say _____ in English

6. They are pieces of _____

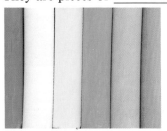

Your guesses: 1 2 3

7. **It's a dictionary.**

1. need/check spelling
2. use/check pronunciation
3. have/find the meaning of words

8. It's a _____

Your guesses: 1 2 3

Your guesses: _____   A's guesses: _____

 **Challenge!**

Take five things from your bag or desk. Imagine. What else could they be? (Example: a pencil could be a microphone or a rocket.) Give hints. **A** will guess.

Places to eat

Do you know of any foods that were named after cities or countries?

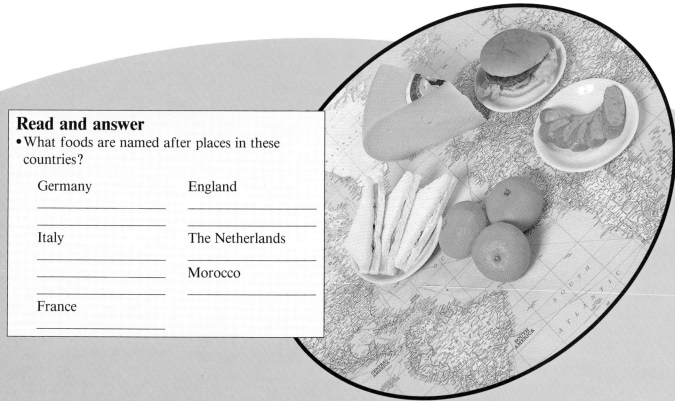

Read and answer
• What foods are named after places in these
 countries?

Germany	England
_____	_____
Italy	The Netherlands
_____	_____
	Morocco
France	_____
_____	

   Foods get their names in many ways. Even the names of countries and cities are
sometimes used for food!

   The best known is the **hamburger**. It was named for Hamburg, a city in Germany.
Do you know of another meat named after a German city? The city is Frankfurt.
The food, of course, is the **frankfurter** sausage we eat as hot dogs. Where do you
think we get the name for **bologna** sausage **sandwiches**? "Bologna" is a place in Italy.
"Sandwich" gets its name from Sandwich, England.

   Many cheeses are named after places. Of course you know where **Swiss** cheese got
its name. Did you know that the **Parmesan** cheese we use to flavor spaghetti and pizza
is named for Parma, Italy? **Cheddar** is a place in England. **Gouda** is in the Netherlands
and **Roquefort** is in France.

   Fruits sometimes have place names, too. **Cantaloupe** melons are named after
Cantalupo, a town in Italy. **Tangerines**—a small fruit something like an orange—
get their name from Tangier, Morocco.

   Are any foods named after places in your country?

Circle the word that doesn't belong.

breakfast	(hungry)	dinner	lunch
use	need	rest	have
chop	build	slice	cut
cook	broil	fry	keep
nail	chopstick	iron	vegetable

Write two more sets.

| ___ | ___ | ___ | ___ |
| ___ | ___ | ___ | ___ |

Check it out!

✓ "I use **it** to cook" means it is for cooking.

✓ "I use**d** to cook" means you don't cook anymore!

Talking to Vince

Vince: What do you think this is for?

You: *Do you use it to* ?

Vince: No. That's not it.

You: *Do* *need* ?

Vince: Wrong. Try again.

You: *have* ?

Vince: That not right either.
Give up?

You: _____

Vince: I use it to make you ask questions!

I enjoy hiking.

Step 1: Listen.
Step 2: Practice.

on weekends   playing tennis
on Sunday   swimming

me, too   play   week
I do, too   swim   weekend

Saturday afternoon
tomorrow

play tennis   like fun
go swimming   great

It's a match!

....

Step 1: Answer the questions.

What do you like to do at home?
• I like _____

What do you dislike doing at home?
• I dislike _____ ing

What do you like to do at school?
• I enjoy _____ ing

What do you dislike doing at school?
• I don't like _____

What do you like to do in your free time?
• I love _____

What do you dislike doing in your free time?
• I don't enjoy _____ ing

What do you want to do in the future?
• I want to _____

What do you hope to do someday?
• I hope to _____

Step 2: Aaron and Jill are on a TV game show.
     Listen. Write their answers.

Aaron   Jill

	Aaron	Jill
At home,	• I like *to cook.*	I like _____ .
	• I dislike _____ *ing* _____ .	I dislike _____ .
At school,	• I enjoy _____ *ing*.	I enjoy _____ .
	• I don't like _____ .	I don't like _____ .
In my free time,	• I love _____ .	I love _____ .
	• I don't enjoy _____ .	I don't enjoy _____ .
Someday,	• I want to _____ .	I want to _____ .
	• I hope to _____ .	I hope to _____ .

How many times did you match Aaron or Jill? _____

Now try Speechwork 6. **A,** look at page 77. **B,** look at page 78.

I like skiing!
I like to ski!

Some verbs take *verb* + *ing*.
     I *enjoy* ski**ing**.
Some verbs take *to* + *verb*.
     I learned **to** ski last year.
Some take either *verb* + *ing* or *to* + *verb*.
     I *like* ski**ing**. I *like* **to** ski.

I	enjoy like		ski**ing**. study**ing**.		I	do, too. don't. don't either.
	like **to** (don't) want **to**		ski. study.			
	learned **to**	read	when I was five.			did, too. didn't.

Step 1: Finish the sentences. Read the sentences to B. Check B's answers.

B's answers:

	Same	Different
☐ I love _____ **ing**.		
☐ I want **to** _____.		
☐ I enjoy _____ **ing**.		
☐ I don't like **to** _____.		
☐ I dislike _____ **ing**.		
☐ I hope **to** _____ in a few years.		
☐ I learned **to** _____ when I was _____. age		
☐ I finished _____ **ing** last month.		
☐ I never start _____ **ing** in the morning.		
☐ I try **to** _____ every _____. day, month, year, etc.		

How do you spell it?

How many times did **B** give the same answer? _____

Step 2: Cover the sentences. Write these verbs in the right boxes.

~~love~~   want   start   like   dislike   hope   learn   finish   enjoy   try

verb + **ing**	either **to** or **ing**	**to** + verb
• •	• *love* •	• •
•	• •	•

Challenge!   Close your book.
                             Can you remember the verbs? Write them.

I like skiing!
I like to ski!

....

Some verbs take *verb* + *ing*.
    I *enjoy* ski**ing**.
Some verbs take *to* + *verb*.
    I *learned* **to** ski last year.
Some take either *verb* + *ing* or *to* + *verb*.
    I *like* ski**ing**. I *like* **to** ski.

I	enjoy / like	skiing. / studying.	I	do, too. / don't. / don't either.
	like **to** / (don't) want **to**	ski. / study.		
	learned **to**	read	when I was five.	did, too. / didn't.

Step 1: Finish the sentences. Read the sentences to A. Check A's answers.

A's answers:

	Same	Different
☐ I want **to** _____ .		
☐ I like _____ **ing**.		
☐ I dislike _____ **ing**.		
☐ I start **to** _____ at ____ : ____ .		
☐ I hope **to** _____ this year.		
☐ I don't enjoy _____ **ing**.		
☐ I love **to** _____ .		
☐ I tried _____ **ing** last _____ .		
☐ I never learned **to** _____ .		
☐ I finished _____ **ing** last week.		

(under "I start to" line: *time*)
(under "I tried ing last" line: day, month, year, etc.)

How do you spell it?

How many times did **A** give the same answer? _____

Step 2: Cover the sentences. Write these verbs in the right boxes.

~~love~~   want   start   like   dislike   hope   learn   finish   enjoy   try

verb + **ing**	either **to** or **ing**	**to** + verb
• •	• *love* •	• •
•	• •	•

Challenge!   Close your book.
Can you remember the verbs? Write them.

Typical Americans

Most teenagers disagree with their parents about some things.
Do you ever disagree with your parents? About what?

Read and answer
- Do American teenagers like or dislike going
  to school?

  _____

- Where do American high school students like
  to go on dates?

  _____

- What do they disagree with their parents about?

  _____

  _____

  _____

What do American students think about school and dating? Are their opinions
the same as yours?

Most American teenagers—over three-fourths—enjoy going to school. About forty
percent say that their teacher is very good. They would give the teacher an "A."
About two-thirds think they have the right amount of homework. Most of the rest
want to have less.

American teenagers like to go out on dates more often than teenagers in other
countries. Twelve percent of students in their last year of high school go out on a date
more than three times a week. They enjoy going to movies, parties, dances and sports
events. About half go on dates at least once a week. Forty-four percent of American
teenage girls have asked a boy for a date. Only a few—(thirteen percent)—high school
seniors never go out on a date.

Of course, what teenagers like doing
and what their parents want them to do
is not always the same.

What do
U.S. teenagers
disagree with
their parents
about?

60 –
50 –
40 –
30 –
20 –
10 –

percent
of U.S.
teenagers   clothes   boyfriends/   staying
                              girlfriends   out late

Finish the sentences. Use **to** or **+ing**. Use **play** or **practice** if you need it.

• I want *to play tennis* today.
(tennis)

• I love _____.
(soccer)

• I start _____ at 8:00 in the morning.
(exercise)

• I enjoy _____.
(karate)

• I like _____.
(ski)

• I dislike _____.
(run)

• I don't like _____.
(wrestle)

• I hope _____ next Saturday.
(judo)

• I learned _____ when I was young.
(swim)

• I finished _____ an hour ago.
(basketball)

Remember:
✔ Team sports need the word **play**:
   I like to play tennis.
   I like playing volleyball.
✔ One-person sports **don't** use play:
   I love to swim.
   I love skiing.
✔ Fighting sports are different:
   Asian fighting sports use **practice**:
   I want to practice karate.
   I enjoy practicing judo.
   Other fighting sports don't use
   practice or **play**:
   I learned to fence last year.
   I dislike boxing.

Check it out!

Talking to Vince

Vince: Let's talk about school.
       What do you like to study?

You: _____.

Vince: Anything else?

You: _____.

Vince: How about math?
       Do you like or dislike studying it?

You: _____.

Vince: I enjoy speaking English but
       don't like doing homework.
       How about you?

You: _____.

_____ *studying?*

Vince: Me? Study?
       My favorite thing in school is LUNCH!

Like this?

Step 1: Listen.
Step 2: Practice.

need to
must

push   can't
move

lift   have to
change

don't
you must not

You can't do that.

....

Do you know these words?   **can   can't   don't   should   shouldn't   have to   don't have to   must**

Listen. This is a dormitory. What are the rules? **Write the words.**

   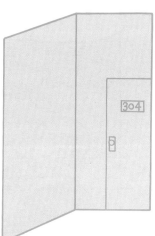

1. You *have to* turn off the music at 11 o'clock.

2. You _____ turn off the lights at 11.

3. You _____ have a pet.

4. You _____ have food in your room.

5. You _____ have a refrigerator.

 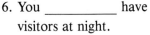  

6. You _____ have visitors at night.

7. _____ use nails or tacks for posters. You _____ use tape.

8. You _____ talk on the phone in the hall at night.

Now try Speechwork 7. **A**, look at page 79. **B**, look at page 80.

Be Careful!

Can Should	I we	turn go	right left north south east west	at the tree? at the fence?	Yes,	you we	can. should. have to.
Do	I we	have to	go turn		No,		can't. shouldn't. don't.

Go through the maze. Be careful. There are monsters you can't see.

Ask B which way you should go. Write your starting time: _____ : _____

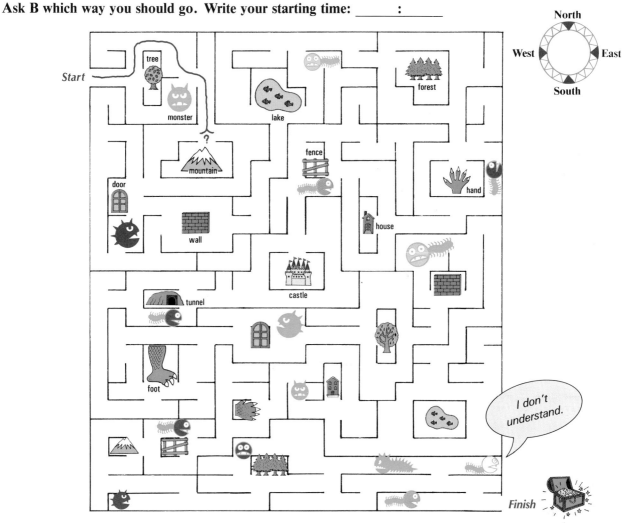

Write your finishing time: _____ : _____   How long did it take? _____

 Close your book. What should you do when you travel?
What shouldn't you do? What do you have to do? Think of 10 things.

Be Careful!

Can Should	I we	turn go	right left north	at the tree?	Yes,	you we	can. should. have to.
Do	I we	**have to**	go turn	south east west	at the fence?	No,		can't. shouldn't. don't.

Go through the maze. Be careful. There are monsters you can't see.
Ask A which way you should go. Write your starting time: _____ : _____

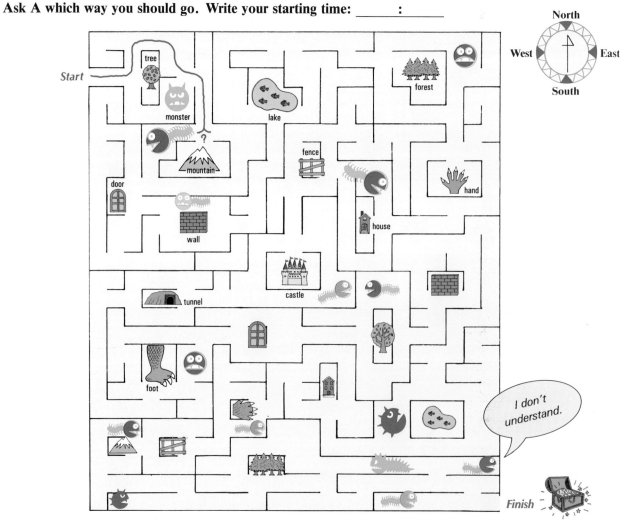

Write your finishing time: _____ : _____   How long did it take? _____

Close your book. What should you do when you travel?
What shouldn't you do? What do you have to do? Think of 10 things.

Be careful!

Have you ever been to a summer camp?
Would you like to work at one?

Read and answer
- What rules did people break?
  What was dangerous?

  _____
  _____
  _____

   A camp counselor is a kind of teacher. Camp counselors are usually college students
who work at camps during the summer. They take care of the children who go to the
camps. They teach them to ride horses, to swim and other things.

Read this letter from a camp counselor to his parents.

August 2

Dear Mom and Dad,

Sorry I haven't written. I've been so busy. The children here are always breaking the camp rules. I have to watch them very closely all the time.

Yesterday, one boy got lost when he went hiking all alone. He didn't take anyone with him. I told him he should always go hiking with another person. We were lucky to find him quickly.

On Tuesday, I saw another boy swimming alone. I told him to get out of the lake. They shouldn't go swimming alone. He was swimming near some boats. That's dangerous too.

Last week, some people from town rode their motorcycles through our camp. That's against the rules. No one got hurt but some of the little kids were afraid of the noise.

There are so many things to be careful about! I'll be happy to get home where I can relax.

Love,

Jerry

Camp Custer
Custer, SD 57023

What do the signs mean?
Write the words: lift   pull   ~~push~~   turn   tunnel

north   south   east   west

You have

to _*push*_ .

You should

_____ this.

You can not

_____ left.

You should

_____ this.

There is

a _____ .

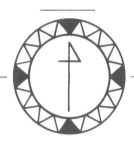

Check it out!

✔ **must** & **have to** mean
   "Do it!"
✔ **must not** means "Don't!"
✔ **don't have to** means
   "You don't have to [but you
   can do it if you want to.]"

Talking
to
Vince

Vince: Does your school have a lot of rules?

You: _____

Vince: What rule do you like?

You: _____

Vince: What rule don't you like?

You: _____

Vince: Really? Do you always follow that rule?

You: _____

_____ _follow the rules?_

Vince: Of course I do. Sometimes.

It's easy to find.

Step 1: Listen.
Step 2: Practice.

Hollywood Theater   post office
Java Coffee Shop   book store

post office
book store

two   on the right
five   in front of you

Where's the video shop?

Step 1: Listen. Where can you do these things? Match the things and the places:

1. rent a movie   *c*
2. buy a cake   _____
3. buy clothes   _____
4. buy a notebook   _____
5. get a dictionary   _____
6. buy a CD player   _____

a. **a department store**
b. **an appliance store**
c. **a video shop**
d. **a bakery**
e. **a stationery store**
f. **a book store**

Step 2: Listen. Follow the directions. Write the places on the maps.

1. a video shop *video shop*

2. a bakery

3. a department store

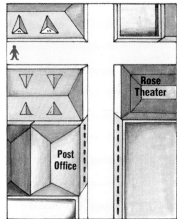

4. a stationery store

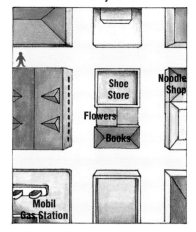

5. a book store

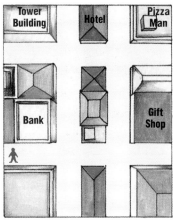

6. an appliance store

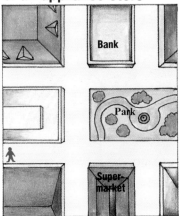

Now try Speechwork 8. **A,** look at page 79. **B,** look at page 80.

How do I get there?

Excuse me.	How do I get to Where's	the bookstore? a bank?
Take Go down	this street that street	to past	Reed Street. the bookstore. the second corner.
		two blocks.
Turn	right left	(at the bank). (at ABC Travel).
It's	on the corner. on the left. next to the gas station. across from the high school.	

Step 1: Ask B how to get to these places:

 •McDonald's   •Star Stationery Store   •Ace Electric   •The Lunch Box   •City Hospital

Follow B's directions. Write the names on the buildings.

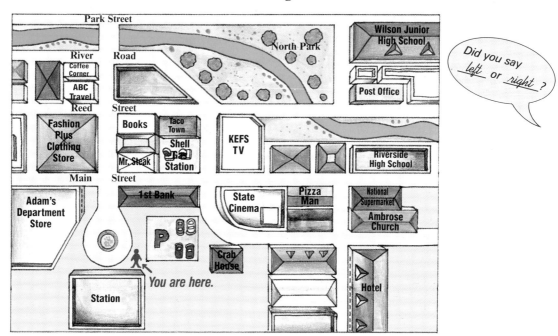

Step 2: Answer B's questions.

Challenge!   Think of places in your city.
Tell **B** how to get to the places. **B** listens and says the places.

How do I get there?

Excuse me.	How do I get to Where's	the bookstore? a bank?	
Take Go down	this street that street	to past	Reed Street. the bookstore. the second corner.
		two blocks.	
Turn	right left	(at the bank). (at ABC Travel).	
It's	on the corner. on the left. next to the gas station. across from the high school.		

Step 1: Answer A's questions.

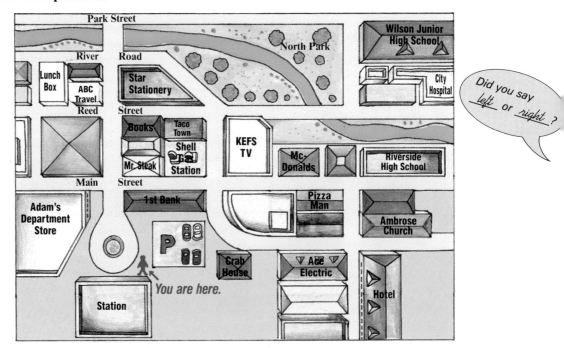

Step 2: Ask A how to get to these places: •National Supermarket   •The Post Office
•Fashion Plus   •The State Cinema   • Coffee Corner

Follow A's directions. Write the names on the buildings.

Challenge!   Think of places in your city.
Tell **A** how to get to the places. **A** listens and says the places.

The Sixth Sense

Have you ever been lost?
How did you find your way home?

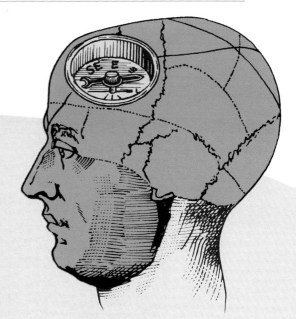

Read and answer
- What is the sixth sense?

  _____

  _____

- Why does a compass point north?

  _____

a compass

Everyone knows about the five senses: sight, hearing, touch, taste and smell. Is there a sixth sense—direction?

The North Pole, the top of the earth, is really a giant magnet. A compass points north because of the North Pole's magnetism. If you put another magnet next to a compass, the compass will point to the magnet. It won't work correctly.

The sixth sense of direction works like a compass. Some people think that we can feel the pull of the North Pole. We may not notice it, but somehow we can feel it. Some people seldom get lost and can easily get to new places because they have a good sense of direction. Maybe they have especially good compasses in their brains. Do you have a strong "sixth sense?"

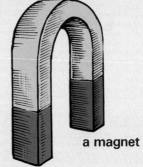

a magnet

Try this!

Work with another student. Put a blindfold over one person's eyes. Turn the person around and around several times. Change your own position, too. Then have your partner stand quietly for about a minute. Ask your partner to point to the front doors of the school building. Repeat this experiment three times. Does your partner have a good sixth sense?

Now try it again. This time, put a magnet next to your partner's head. Could your partner point to the doors? If not, perhaps the magnet stopped your partner's sixth sense.

What are these shops?
Write the names.

> ✔ "Turn **to** the left" says which way to go.
>
> ✔ "It's **on** the left" says where it is.

Talking to Vince

Check it out!

Draw a map that shows your school and your house.

Vince: I want to go to your house after school. How do I get there?

You: _____
_____ .

Vince: OK, then what?

You: _____
_____ .

Vince: I see. After that?

You: _____
_____ .

Vince: I understand. What do I do next?

You: _____
_____ .

Vince: OK, I understand.

You: *Where's* _____ *house?*

Vince: I don't know. I'm lost.
That's why I'm going to your house!

What were you doing at 8:30?

Step 1: Listen.
Step 2: Practice.

Did you feel the earthquake last night?

No. Was there an earthquake?

hear the thunder   a storm
hear the sirens   an accident

You didn't notice it?
It was a big one.

Hmm.
I didn't feel anything.

bad   hear
terrible   notice

Excuse me?

Really? What were you doing at 8:30?
I said, "What were you doing at 8:30?"

Ah...I was watching T.V.

10:45   reading a book
11:00   listening to music

I guess you were watching a good show.

I'm sorry?
Were you saying
something?

reading a terrific book   excuse me
listening to great music   pardon

I was visiting relatives.

....

What were you doing...

  ...at this time last Sunday? _____

  ...on December 31st last year? _____

  ...on a day when you heard some good news? _____

  ...on the happiest day of the past year? _____

Listen.
What were they doing? Write the names.

1. What were you doing at this time last Sunday?

  _____ I was watching TV.

  Emi I was watching a movie.

  _____ I was reading the newspaper.

2. What were you doing on December 31st last year?

  _____ I was visiting relatives.

  _____ I was skiing.

  _____ I was swimming. I went to Hawaii
        during the holiday.

Emi

3. What was some good news for you recently?

  _____ I could visit my cousin in Canada.

  _____ I could work at McDonald's this summer.

  _____ I could go to the college I wanted.

4. What were you doing when you heard the good news?

  _____ I was talking to a teacher.

  _____ I was doing homework.

  _____ I was eating dinner.

5. What were you doing on the happiest day of the past year?

  _____ I was giving a speech. (I won third prize.)

  _____ I was playing soccer. (I kicked the winning goal.)

  _____ I was visiting America. (I met my homestay family.)

Dan

Now try Speechwork 9. **A,** look at page 81. **B,** look at page 82.

What were you doing?

What **were** you do**ing** Where were you	when you met your best friend? when you heard some good news? at midnight on Dec. 31 last year?	I **was**	play**ing** tennis. watch**ing** TV.
			visit**ing** relatives.
Who were you with?		I **was**	with my brother. alone.
		I don't remember.	

Step 1: Answer B's questions.
       Ask B.
       Write B's answers.

	What B was doing:	**Where B was:**	**Who B was with:**
...at midnight on Dec. 31 last year?			
...during your worst moment in school?			
...when you heard some very bad news?			
...when you heard about _____? (important news event)			
...at this time last Sunday?			

Step 2: Write two more questions. Ask B.

- _____

- _____

Challenge!   What was **B**'s most interesting answer? Ask 5 more questions about the topic.

What were you doing?

What **were** you do**ing** Where were you	when you met your best friend? when you heard some good news? at midnight on Dec. 31 last year?	I **was**	play**ing** tennis. watch**ing** TV. visit**ing** relatives.
Who were you with?		I **was**	with my brother. alone.
			I don't remember.

Step 1: Answer A's questions.
Ask A.
Write A's answers.

	What A was doing:	**Where A was:**	**Who A was with:**
...at 12 o'clock noon on Christmas last year?			
...during your best moment in school?			
...when you heard some very good news?			
...when you heard _____ died. **(famous person)**			
...at this time last Sunday?			

Step 2: Write two more questions. Ask A.

- _____

- _____

 **Challenge!**   What was **A**'s most interesting answer?
Ask 5 more questions about the topic.

Earthquake!

Have you ever felt a big earthquake?
When? What happened?

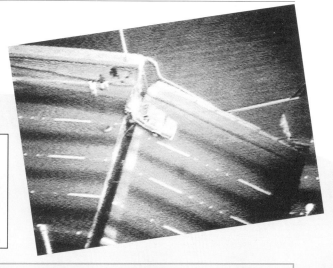

Read and answer

- How did the man feel during the earthquake?

  _____

  _____

- What did the woman do to help?

  _____

If you've ever been in a big earthquake, you know how dangerous they can be. If there is an earthquake, there are several things you should remember.

During an earthquake-
- Don't run outside. Get under a door or a table.
- Don't use elevators. They may stop.
- Don't drive. The police and fire department need the roads.
- Don't use the phones. They are needed for emergencies.
- Most important, **stay calm**.

Ask the people

What were you doing when last Friday's earthquake started?

Bill Evans
Office worker

I was walking to lunch. At first I didn't feel anything. Then I saw things falling down. Some windows broke in the stores near my office. There was broken glass everywhere. I was really scared. Some people were running but most people were calm. They were helping each other.

Ellen Frank
Theater manager

I was getting ready for work. I heard some yelling in the elevator in my apartment building. Some high school boys were in the elevator and the door wouldn't open. I tried calling the police but the phone didn't work. I talked to the boys and tried to calm them down. The building manager got them out about an hour later. I was late for work but I was happy to help.

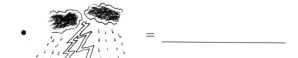

Write the words.

• very good = _great_

• not frightened = _c_ _____

• 12 o'clock at night = _m_ _____

•  = _____

• wonderful = _t_ _____

•  = _____

• bad, worse, _____

•  = _____

• very bad = _____

• _____ = _____

Find the words.

```
F I N D Z O
A T C Y N B
C H P W A S
S E L U R R
M W E Y C X
N I O N K T
A E R R T O
C P Y U D T
U I H G C S
```

```
S T A T O M M O G A G R O D
T R E E R I G H R C R L R M
O E A R T H Q U A K E E A L I
R Y T R R Z E B T G A T F O D
M H Q I W I I P A C T A I N
U B U B O R F O R T A B L I
M C A L R H Z I O I U L A G
S A J E S O R L C N Z O M H
F I T O T M A C C I D E N T
```

Check it out!

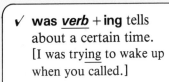

✓ **was _verb_ + ing** tells about a certain time. [I was trying to wake up when you called.]

✓ **_verb_ + ed** tells about once or more than once. [I tried to get up early today. I tried yesterday, too!]

Talking to Vince

Vince: What were you doing at 6 o'clock last night?

You: _____.

Vince: Oh. How about at 8 o'clock?

You: _____.

Vince: And at 10?

You: _____.

Vince: Really? What were you doing at midnight?

You: _____.

Vince: Oh. I see.

You: _What_ _____
_____ _last night?_

Vince: Me? I was thinking of questions.

Who's that?

 Step 1: Listen.
Step 2: Practice.

woman flowered
        striped

orange   yellow blouse
red   checked scarf

she's science
       math

she   her awful
                        terrible

Fashion show.

Step 1: What are these patterns called?
Listen. Write the words:

checked, flowered, plaid, plain, polka dot, solid, striped

1. *striped*   2. _____   3. _____   4 _____   5. _____   6. _____

                                                                    or _____

Step 2: Listen to the fashion show.
Draw the patterns.

Now try Speechwork 10. **A**, look at page 81. **B**, look at page 82.

What's she wearing?

Her His	skirt jacket	is	plaid. blue.		Is it	long or short? solid or striped?
	pants tie	are	checked.			light or dark? big or small dots?
		has	polka dots.		Are they	
She He	is wearing a has a	long short-sleeved	dress. shirt.			

Tell B about the clothes in the blue box. B will draw them.

Ask about the clothes in the yellow box. Draw them.

Look at page 58. Are your drawings the same? _____

Challenge!	Close your book. Tell **B** about your favorite clothes. **B** will draw them.

What's she wearing?

Her His	skirt jacket	is	plaid. blue. checked.		Is it	long or short? solid or striped? light or dark? big or small dots?
	pants tie	are				
		has	polka dots.			
She He	is wearing a has a	long short-sleeved	dress. shirt.	Are they		

Ask about the clothes in the yellow box. Draw them.

Tell A about the clothes in the blue box. A will draw them.

Excuse me?

Look at page 57. Are your drawings the same? _____

 Close your book.
Tell **A** about your favorite clothes. **A** will draw them.

Japanese Fashion

Do you like designer brand clothes?
Which designers do you like best?

Read and answer

- Are Yoji Yamamoto and Rei Kawakubo traditional or modern designers?

  _____

- Find two unusual ideas about clothing.

  _____

  _____

The first Japanese fashion designers who became famous in the United States and Europe were Hanae Mori and Kenzo Takada. After that, Issey Miyake's beautiful and unusual clothes became popular. Several other designers have become famous more recently.

YOJI YAMAMOTO

Yoji Yamamoto lived in Paris in the 1960's, but returned to Tokyo and worked with his mother, who made dresses. Now he thinks those dresses were too traditional. He thinks the women who wore them were traditional, too.

Yamamoto believes that wearing different kinds of clothes can change a person's life. He wants people to look at his clothes and have strong feelings. In the past, he made a lot of black clothes. Recently, he's been making men's clothes that look like sports uniforms.

REI KAWAKUBO

Rei Kawakubo likes to challenge the way people think about clothes. Her company is called *Comme de Garçons.* The name is French. It means "like the boys." Even though she makes clothes for both men and women, she thinks they don't have to look the way men's and women's clothes usually do. For example, Kawakubo's jackets often look different than most jackets. They might have two or three layers of cloth on the back—or no back at all!

There are many other popular Japanese designers. Kansai Yamamoto, Yoshie Inaba, Mitsuhiro Matsuda and Mariko Koga are all making fashion news. Japanese fashion is not just for Japan, anymore. Top designers have shops from Manhattan to Manila and from Taipei to Toronto. Japanese fashion is everywhere!

What are they wearing?
Write the words.

He's wearing a _striped_ tie,
a gray _____ _____ and
a _____ jacket.

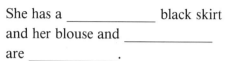

She has a _____ black skirt
and her blouse and _____
are _____.

Her blouse is _____
Her hat and bag are _____.

His pants are _____ and
he has a _____ - _____ shirt.

Check it out!

✓ You **put on** clothes
  in the morning.
✓ You are **wearing**
  clothes now.
  [I'm putting on my sweater.
  Vince is wearing his pajamas.]

𝕿alking
  to
𝖁ince

Vince: What kind of clothes do you like?

You: _____.

Vince: Tell me about your favorite shirt.

You: _____.

Vince: How about the sweater you like best?

You: _____.

Vince: Your favorite pants?

You: _____.

Vince: Are there any kinds of clothes you don't like?

You: _I don't_ _____.

What kind _____

_____ _you like?_

Vince: My favorite clothes?
  I like my pink polka dot pajamas the best!

This one?

 Step 1: Listen.
Step 2: Practice.

school
camp

boy   in   blue suit
man   that has   big sweater
woman

he

dislike   him
can't stand

My family.

....

Step 1:
Look at the picture.
Listen. Write the numbers.

1. The man with the blue shirt is my uncle.   *1*

2. The woman who is holding the baby is my grandmother.   _____

3. My aunt is the woman in the striped shirt.   _____

4. The man who has the beard is my father.   _____

5. The boy with the short hair is my brother.   _____

Step 2:
Two people are talking about the picture.
Listen. Write the names:

Chris,   Dave,   John,   Kent,   Larry,   Mary,   Mia,   Peter,   Vicki

Now try Speechwork 11. **A,** look at page 83. **B,** look at page 84.

Vince's family

Which one is his	mother? father? cousin? sister?		The	tall heavy set	woman man boy girl	with that has who has	the hat a moustache a backpack short hair	is Vince's is his	mom. father. cousin. sister.
What is her	dress basket	like?	It's the		one basket		that is striped. which has food in it.		

This is Vince's family.
Find the missing people.
Ask B what they look like.

Vince's
grandmother

Find his
grandfather

Find his
aunt

Vince's
uncle

SUCCESS

Vince's
mother
(mom)

Vince's
father
(dad)

Find his
cousin

I don't understand.

Vince's mother

Vince's
sister

Vince

Find his
brother

BUS STOP

Challenge!   Close your book.
Describe teachers in your school. **B** will guess who you are thinking of.

Vince's family

Which one is his	mother? father? cousin? sister?		The	tall heavy set	woman man boy girl	with that has who has	the hat a moustache a backpack short hair	is Vince's is his	mom. father. cousin. sister.
What is her	dress basket	like?	It's the		one basket		that is striped. which has food in it.		

This is Vince's family.
Find the missing people.
Ask A what they look like.

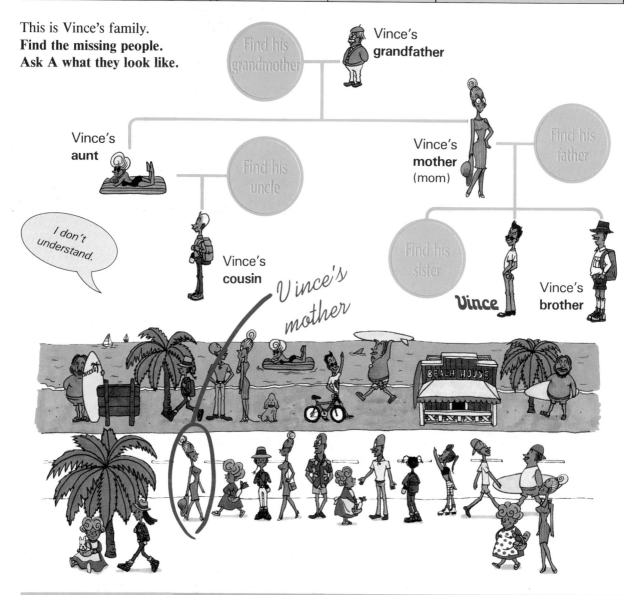

Challenge!
Close your book.
Describe teachers in your school. **A** will guess who you are thinking of.

Singapore Weddings

Have you ever been to a wedding?
What do people do at weddings in your country?

bride
groom

Read and answer
- Find something that is the same about
  Malay and Indian weddings.

  _____

  _____

- Find something that is the same about
  Chinese and Malay weddings.

  _____

  _____

Singapore is made up of many kinds of
people. The largest groups are Chinese, Malays
and Indians. Each group has its own special
marriage customs.

Chinese weddings. Before the wedding, the
bride's and groom's mothers comb the wedding
couple's hair. The bride and groom serve tea
to the groom's parents, aunts and uncles. Then
they go to the bride's family's house to give
gifts. After that they go to a park to take
photographs. They ride in a car with red, pink
and gold ribbons. In the evening, there is a big
dinner. The women wear pink or gold dresses
because those are lucky colors. The bride
usually wears a red or pink dress at the dinner.

Malay weddings. Malay weddings last two
days in the city and many days in the country.
On the first day, a Saturday evening, the bride
and groom sign the marriage certificate—the
paper that means they are really married. On
Sunday morning, the couple greets their friends,
who throw yellow rice over the bride and groom
to wish them luck. In the evening, there is
a big dinner. Guests get a basket which is filled
with hard-boiled eggs to take home.

Indian weddings. A tree is planted at an
Indian wedding. After the couple plants the
tree, they change clothes. The bride wears
clothes the groom gives her. The man ties a
necklace around the woman's neck. Guests
throw rice at the couple to wish them luck.
Guests do not wear black or white. Bright
colors are the best for weddings.

Memory test

This is a memory test.
Look at Vince's family on pages 63-64.
Look for exactly 2 minutes.
Finish the sentences.

• The woman who has the basket is Vince's *grandmother*.

   • The man with the sweater is Vince's _____.

• The boy that has a brown backpack is his _____.

   • The woman with the striped dress is his _____.

• The man with the swimming suit is Vince's _____.

   • The man with the white long-sleeved shirt is his _____.

• The child with the hat is his _____.

   • The woman with the dark glasses is his _____.

• The man with the short-sleeved shirt is his _____.

Check it out!

✔ Use **who** for people.
✔ **That** is for both people and things.

Talking to Vince

Draw a picture of you and two friends.

Vince: Who's this?

You: _____ *one?*

Vince: The one who's on the right.

You: *That's* _____ .

Vince: How about the person who's on the left?

You: *That's* _____ .

Vince: They look really nice.

You: *They* _____ .
Do you have any pictures?

Vince: Pictures? No.
I broke my camera.

What's this place like?

Step 1: Listen.
Step 2: Practice.

Hi. I'm new here. Can <u>I ask you about the company</u>?

<u>Sure</u>.

you help me
I ask you something

OK
of course

<u>Should I</u> get here before 9?

You <u>don't have to</u>.

do I have to
do I need to

should try to
really should

Do we have a lot of <u>breaks</u>?

<u>I think so</u>.

vacations
holidays

enough
yes, we do

Do you like working here?

Yes. I'm the boss.

I do. How about you?

....

Step 1: Listen. Check (✓) the words.
Circle the answers for yourself.

1. He ☑ has   a **bike**.
   ☐ doesn't have
   •I do, too.   •I don't.

2. She ☐ has   a **watch**.
   ☐ doesn't have
   •I do.   •I don't, either.

3. He ☐ likes   to **play tennis**.
   ☐ doesn't like
   •I do, too.   •I don't.

4. She ☐ likes   to **ski**.
   ☐ doesn't like
   •I do.   •I don't, either.

5. He ☐ could   **run faster** 5 years ago.
   ☐ couldn't
   •I could, too.   •I couldn't.

6. She ☐ could   **use a computer** 5 years ago.
   ☐ couldn't
   •I could.   •I couldn't, either.

7. He ☐ should **speak English** in class.
   ☐ always **speaks**
   •I should, too.   •I do, too.

8. She ☐ should   **watch TV**...
   ☐ shouldn't
   •I don't.   •I shouldn't, either.

Step 2: Listen.
Are the people the same or different?
Circle the answers.

1.	same	(different)		5.	same	different
2.	same	different		6.	same	different
3.	same	different		7.	same	different
4.	same	different		8.	same	different

Now try Speechwork 12. **A**, look at page 83. **B**, look at page 84.

And...

Tell me about		something (else)		you	(don't) have. (don't) like. can('t) do.	I (don't) have a CD. I (don't) like pizza. I can('t) type.
What are	two things		you	**could** do **couldn't** do	5 years ago?	I **could** run faster **and** type. I **couldn't** run as fast **or** type.
				should do **shouldn't** do	more often? so often?	I **should** study **and** read more. I **shouldn't** watch TV **or** movies so often.

Step 1: Ask about B. Write B's answers.

Circle the things that are true for you. Answer B's questions.

B has... ――――― ―――――	**B** doesn't have... ――――― ―――――
B likes... ――――― ―――――	**B** doesn't like... ――――― ―――――
B can... ――――― ―――――	**B** can't... ――――― ―――――
5 years ago, **B** could... ――――― ―――――	5 years ago, **B** couldn't... ――――― ―――――
Things **B** should do more often: ――――― ―――――	Things **B** shouldn't do so often: ――――― ―――――

How do you spell it?

Did you say should or shouldn't?

Step 2: Answer B's questions.

How many things did you circle? ―――――

How many things did **B** circle? ―――――

Total (you + **B**) ―――――

30-40 = You and B are a lot alike.
15-29 = Most people get 15-29.
 0-14 = You and B are very different.

 ***Challenge!***   Close your book. Ask 5 more questions.
Use these words: **who   what   where   when   how   why**

And...

Tell me about	something (else)	you	(don't) have. (don't) like. can('t) do.	I (don't) have a CD. I (don't) like pizza. I can('t) type.
What are	two things	you	**could** do **couldn't** do	5 years ago?	I **could** run faster **and** type. I **couldn't** run as fast **or** type.
			should do **shouldn't** do	more often? so often?	I **should** study **and** read more. I **shouldn't** watch TV **or** movies so often.

Step 1: Ask about A. Write A's answers.
Circle the things that are true for you. Answer A's questions.

A has...
_____
_____

A doesn't have...
_____
_____

How do you spell i̲t̲?

A likes...
_____
_____

A doesn't like...
_____
_____

A can...
_____
_____

A can't...
_____
_____

5 years ago, **A** could...
_____
_____

5 years ago, **A** couldn't...
_____
_____

Did you say should̲ or shouldn't̲?

Things **A** should do
more often:
_____
_____

Things **A** shouldn't do
so often:
_____
_____

Step 2: Answer A's questions.
How many things did you circle? _____
How many things did **A** circle? _____
Total (you + **A**) _____

30-40 = You and A are a lot alike.
15-29 = Most people get 15-29.
 0-14 = You and A are very different.

Challenge!   Close your book. Ask 5 more questions.
Use these words: **who   what   where   when   how   why**

Tom Cruise

Do you have a special dream?
Is there something you really want to do?

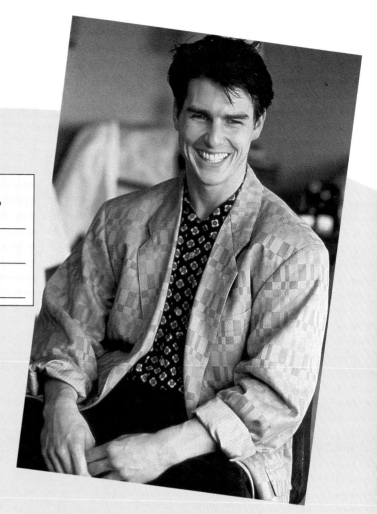

Read and answer
• What problem did Tom Cruise have as a child?
_____

• When did he become an actor?
_____

• Was his life always successful?
_____

When he was a boy, Tom Cruise could not read. He couldn't understand the words. Sometimes they seemed backward to him. Because he couldn't read, he didn't do well in school.

Now, Tom Cruise loves to learn. He carries a dictionary with him and tries to learn new words every day. He looks for new challenges and tries to learn new things. Sometimes he learns new things for movies. He learned to fly a jet for Top Gun and he learned to drive a race car for another movie. He is very interested in the environment. He tries to find out information about environmental problems.

Tom Cruise was born on July 3, 1962. His last name was Mapother, but he changed it. "Tom" is his real first name and "Cruise" is his real middle name. He has three sisters, two older and one younger. His family moved a lot when he was young. He made new friends through sports.

Tom hurt his leg in high school, so he had to stop sports. When he stopped wrestling, he tried acting in a musical play. He was a success. He began to make movies. In Rain Man and The Color of Money, he worked with famous actors. They said that Tom was a very good actor. If he had not hurt his leg in high school, maybe he wouldn't have become an actor. Maybe he would have become a wrestler!

VOCABULARY

Finish the letter.
Use these words: ago   alike   boss   breaks   different
                        holidays   questions   should   shouldn't   vacation

There are two extra words.

Nov. 7

Dear Allan,

   Sorry. I _____ write more often
but I'm very busy. I started a new job
two weeks _____. It is very _____
than my old job. I had a lot of _____
at first but the _____ answered them.
I have two _____ every day and get a
three-week _____ every summer. Of
course, I don't have to work on _____
like Christmas and New Year's.

   I like the job and am learning a lot.

   Love,

   Mia

Remember!

✔ English isn't just for
   practice.
   It's for **communicating!**

Talking to Vince

Vince: I have a CD. Do you have one?

You: _____.

Vince: I listen to music about five hours
       every day.

You: _____ *shouldn't*
     _____.

Vince: I know. But I don't watch TV
       very much. How about you?

You: _____.

Vince: What else do you like?

You: _____
     _____ *like?*

Vince: Me? Well, I like you.

Speechwork 1A

🔊 **Listen and say.**
What's your **name**?
When do you **get up**?
Who's your favorite **singer**?

Where do you **live**?
How do you **get** to **school**?

Listen and say. Finish the sentences.
1. _____ do you **go** to **school**?
2. _____ your favorite _____?
3. _____ his **name**?

👥 **Work with B.**
Say these sentences.

Answer B.
Write the first word B says.

1. **Where** do you **live**?
2. **What's** your favorite **sport**?
3. **When** do you **go** to **bed**?
4. **How** do you **get** to school?
5. **Who's** your favorite TV star?

1. *What's*
2. _____
3. _____
4. _____
5. _____

Speechwork 2A

🔊 **Listen and say.**
fast → faster   pretty → prettier   popular → more popular
●   ● ●   ● ● ●

How many syllables in each word? Write your answers.

funny *2*   silly ____   cute ____   beautiful ____
● ●

👥 **Work with B.**
Say each word two times.

1. popular   2. fast   3. noisy   4. smart   5. beautiful   6. friendly
● ● ●   ●   ● ●   ●   ● ● ●   ● ●

How many syllables? Write your answers.
1. _____   2. _____   3. _____   4. _____   5. _____   6. _____

Speechwork 1B

Listen and say.
What's your **name**?
When do you **get up**?
Who's your favorite **singer**?

Where do you **live**?
How do you **get** to **school**?

Listen and say. Finish the sentences.
1. _____ do you **go** to **school**?
2. _____ your favorite _____?
3. _____ his **name**?

Work with A.

Answer B.
Write the first word B says.

1. *Where*
2. _____
3. _____
4. _____
5. _____

Say these sentences.

1. **What's** your favorite **food**?
2. **How** do you **get** to school?
3. **Who** is your favorite **singer**?
4. **Where** do you **live**?
5. **When** do you **get up**?

Speechwork 2B

Listen and say.
fast → faster   pretty → prettier   popular → more popular

How many syllables in each word? Write your answers.

funny _2_   silly ____   cute ____   beautiful ____

Work with A.
How many syllables? Write your answers.
1. _____ 2. _____ 3. _____ 4. _____ 5. _____ 6. _____

Say each word two times.

1. intelligent   2. heavy   3. loud   4. dangerous   5. silly   6. big

Speechwork 3A

 Listen and say.
Do you like rock or jazz?
Do you like rock, jazz or classical?

Listen and say. Draw arrows (→).
Do you like cats or dogs?
Do you like cats, dogs or birds?

Work with B.
Say these sentences.
1. Do you like being busy or having nothing to do?
2. Do you like the country or big cities?
3. Do you like beef, fish or chicken?
4. Do you like reading magazines or books?

Finish the sentences.
1. Do you like _____ or _____?
2. Do you like visiting the _____ or visiting the _____?
3. Do you like _____, _____ or _____?
4. Do you like _____ or _____?

Say these sentences.
1. Do you like traveling by plane, train or car?
2. Do you like love stories, horror stories or mysteries?

Listen. Draw arrows (→).
1. Do you like spring, summer, fall or winter?
2. Do you like walking, riding a bicycle or taking a bus?

Speechwork 4A

 Listen and say.
I'm **going** to the **store**.
I'm going to **read** tonight.

Finish these sentences.
I'm _____ to the park.
I'm going to _____ volleyball.
I'm going to _____ my relatives.

Work with B.
Finish these sentences.
1. I'm going to _____ this winter.
2. He's going to _____ this spring.
3. She's _____ to _____.
4. She's going to _____ next week.

Say these sentences.
1. He's going to **play** soccer.
2. She's **going** to **China**.
3. I'm going to **watch** a video.
4. He's **going** to a **movie**.

How do you spell _____?

Speechwork 3B

Listen and say.
Do you like rock or jazz?
Do you like rock, jazz or classical?

Listen and say. Draw arrows (→).
Do you like cats or dogs?
Do you like cats, dogs or birds?

Work with A.

Finish these sentences.
1. Do you like being _____ or having nothing _____ ?
2. Do you like the _____ or _____ ?
3. Do you like _____ , _____ or _____ ?
4. Do you like reading _____ or _____ ?

Say these sentences.
1. Do you like summer or fall?
2. Do you like visiting the ocean or visiting the mountains?
3. Do you like comedies, mysteries or love stories?
4. Do you like Saturday or Sunday?

Listen. Draw arrows (→).
1. Do you like traveling by plane, train or car?
2. Do you like love stories, horror stories or mysteries?

Say these sentences.
1. Do you like spring, summer, fall or winter?
2. Do you like walking, riding a bicycle or taking a bus?

Speechwork 4B

Listen and say.
I'm **going** to the **store**.
I'm going to **read** tonight.

Finish these sentences.
I'm _____ to the park.
I'm going to _____ volleyball.
I'm going to _____ my relatives.

Work with A.

Say these sentences.
1. I'm going to **go skiing** this winter.
2. He's going to **graduate** this spring.
3. She's **going to Canada**.
4. She's going to **get married** next week.

Finish these sentences.
1. He's going to _____ soccer.
2. She's _____ to _____ .
3. I'm going to _____ a video.
4. He's _____ to a _____ .

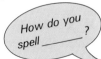
How do you spell _____ ?

Speechwork 5A

🔊 **Listen and say.**

I use it to **cook**. [yes]

I **don't** use it to **cook**. I use it to **teach**. [no]

Listen and say. Yes or no? Check (✓) your answers.

1...cook food.   ☐ yes   ☐ no

2...keep things cold.   ☐ yes   ☐ no

👥 **Work with B.**

Finish these sentences.

1. I use it to keep things _____ .
2. She uses it to _____ .
3. She _____ need it to go _____ .
4. I want it to _____ .
5. He _____ use it to _____ .
6. He _____ need it to _____ .

Say these sentences.

1. I need it to play **soccer**.
2. He uses it to **exercise**.
3. He **doesn't** need it to play **volleyball**.
4. She needs it to **draw**.
5. She **doesn't** use it to **cook**.
6. I want it to keep things **hot**.

Speechwork 6A

🔊 **Listen and say.**

I like to ski.   **I** don't.

I enjoy skiing.   I do **too**.

Listen and say. Check (✓) your answers.

I like to travel.   ☐ same   ☐ different

I like studying.   ☐ same   ☐ different

👥 **Work with B.**

Answer B. Choose one.

	same	different
1.	☐ I don't **either**.	☐ **I** do.
2.	☐ I do **too**.	☐ **I** don't.
3.	☐ I do **too**.	☐ **I** don't.
4.	☐ I don't **either**.	☐ **I** do.
5.	☐ I do **too**.	☐ **I** don't.
6.	☐ I do **too**.	☐ **I** don't.

Say these sentences.

1. I dislike reading.
2. I enjoy cooking.
3. I don't enjoy traveling.
4. I love to study.
5. I want to go to Europe.
6. I hope to study in the United States.

Speechwork 5B

🔊 **Listen and say.**
I use it to **cook**. [yes]
I **don't** use it to **cook**. I use it to **teach**. [no]

Listen and say. Yes or no? Check (✓) your answers.
1...cook food.   ☐ yes   ☐ no
2...keep things cold.   ☐ yes   ☐ no

👥 **Work with A.**

Say these sentences.
1. I use it to keep things **cold**.
2. She uses it to **play tennis**.
3. She **doesn't** need it to go **skiing**.
4. I want it to **bake**.
5. He **doesn't** use it to **write**.
6. He **doesn't** need it to **teach**.

Finish these sentences.
1. I need it to play _____.
2. He uses it to _____.
3. He _____ need it to play _____.
4. She needs it to _____.
5. She _____ use it to _____.
6. I want it to keep things _____.

Speechwork 6B

🔊 **Listen and say.**
I like to ski.   **I** don't.
I enjoy skiing.   I do **too**.

Listen and say. Check (✓) your answers.
I like to travel.   ☐ same   ☐ different
I like studying.   ☐ same   ☐ different

👥 **Work with A.**
Say these sentences.

1. I don't like to play tennis.
2. I dislike driving.
3. I want to learn Spanish.
4. I don't enjoy skiing.
5. I hope to go to Africa.
6. I like movies.

Answer A. Choose one.

same	different
1. ☐ I do **too**.	☐ **I don't.**
2. ☐ I do **too**.	☐ **I don't.**
3. ☐ I don't **either**.	☐ **I do.**
4. ☐ I do **too**.	☐ **I don't.**
5. ☐ I do **too**.	☐ **I don't.**
6. ☐ I do **too**.	☐ **I don't.**

Speechwork 7A

 Listen and say.

You can't do that.   I can't do that?
You shouldn't be here.   I shouldn't be here?

Are these questions? Check (✓) your answers.

1. ☐...read this?   ☐ ...read this.   3. ☐ ...ask him?   ☐...ask him.
2. ☐...be here?   ☐...be here.   4. ☐ ...do that?   ☐...do that.

 Work with B.

Say these sentences.
I can't do that.
I can't have one?
I shouldn't be here.

Up or down? Draw arrows (→).
I have to listen.
I should buy this?
I don't have to read this.

Say these sentences.

1. You can understand that?
2. She doesn't have to go.
3. You want a pet?
4. You shouldn't do that.
5. I don't have to.

Are these questions?
Check (✓) your answers.

1. ☐ have to?   ☐...have to.
2. ☐ go there?   ☐ go there.
3. ☐ use nails?   ☐ use nails.
4. ☐ see her?   ☐ see her.
5. ☐ the music?   ☐ the music.

Speechwork 8A

 Listen and say.
Turn right, then left.
Turn left, left again, and right.

Listen and say. Draw arrows (→).
Turn left, then right.
Turn left, right, and left again.

 Work with B.

Say these sentences.
1. Turn left, then right.
2. Walk straight two blocks, turn left, then right.
3. Go right, left, and right again.
4. Walk three blocks and turn left.
5. Turn right, right again, and left.
6. It's straight ahead on the right.

Listen. Draw arrows (→).
1. Go left, right, and left again.
2. Walk two blocks and turn left.
3. Turn right, then left.
4. It's straight ahead on the left.
5. Turn left, left again, and right.
6. Walk three blocks, turn right, then left.

Speechwork 7B

Listen and say.

You can't do that.
You shouldn't be here.

I can't do that?
I shouldn't be here?

Are these questions? Check (✓) your answers.

1. ☐ ...read this?   ☐ ...read this.   3. ☐ ...ask him?   ☐ ...ask him.
2. ☐ ...be here?   ☐ ...be here.   4. ☐ ...do that?   ☐ ...do that.

Work with A.

Up or down? Draw arrows (→).

I can't do that.
I can't have one?
I shouldn't be here.

Say these sentences.

I have to listen.
I should buy this?
I don't have to read this.

Are these questions?
Check (✓) your answers.

1. ☐ understand that?   ☐ understand that.
2. ☐ have to go?   ☐ have to go.
3. ☐ a pet?   ☐ a pet.
4. ☐ do that?   ☐ do that.
5. ☐ have to?   ☐ have to.

Say these sentences.

1. We have to?
2. I shouldn't go there.
3. Don't use nails.
4. We can't see her?
5. We have to turn off the music?

Speechwork 8B

Listen and say.

Turn right, then left.
Turn left, left again, and right.

Listen and say. Draw arrows (→).

Turn left, then right.
Turn left, right, and left again.

Work with A.

Listen. Draw arrows (→).

1. Turn left, then right.
2. Walk straight two blocks, turn left, then right.
3. Go right, left, and right again.
4. Walk three blocks and turn left.
5. Turn right, right again, and left.
6. It's straight ahead on the right.

Say these sentences.

1. Go left, right, and left again.
2. Walk two blocks and turn left.
3. Turn right, then left.
4. It's straight ahead on the left.
5. Turn left, left again, and right.
6. Walk three blocks, turn right, then left.

Speechwork 9A

 Listen and say.
What were you doing on **Friday**?
I was going to school. What were **you** doing on Friday?

Listen and say. Circle the loudest word.
What were you doing on Wednesday?
What were you doing on Wednesday?

 Work with B.

Say these sentences.
1. What were you doing on **January 1**?
2. What were **you** doing on Thursday?
3. What were you doing last **summer vacation**?
4. What were you doing on your **birthday**?
5. What were **you** doing last night?
6. What were **you** doing?

Circle the loudest word.
1. What were you doing?
2. What were you doing on December 1?
3. What were you doing on Monday?
4. What were you doing on your birthday?
5. What were you doing last winter vacation?
6. What were you doing last night?

Speechwork 10A

 Listen and say.
Is it **big** or **small**?   It's **small**.
Are they **dark** or **light**?   They're **light**.

Listen and say. Check (✓) the answer.
Is the shirt **striped** or **plaid**?   ☐ striped   ☐ plaid
Are the boots **big** or **small**?   ☐ big   ☐ small

 Work with B.

Ask B. Check (✓) B's answer.
1. Is the shirt **big** or **small**?   ☐ big   ☐ small
2. Is it **solid** or **striped**?   ☐ solid   ☐ striped
3. Are the stripes **gray** or **black**? ☐ gray   ☐ black

4. Is the skirt **plaid** or **flowered**? ☐ plaid   ☐ flowered
5. Is it **long** or **short**?   ☐ long   ☐ short
6. Is it **dark** or **light**?   ☐ dark   ☐ light

**Listen to B's questions.
Answer B.**

Speechwork 9B

📻 **Listen and say.**
What were you doing on **Friday**?
I was going to school. What were **you** doing on Friday?

Listen and say. Circle the loudest word.
What were you doing on Wednesday?
What were you doing on Wednesday?

👥 **Work with A.**

Circle the loudest word.
1. What were you doing on January 1?
2. What were you doing on Thursday?
3. What were you doing last summer vacation?
4. What were you doing on your birthday?
5. What were you doing last night?
6. What were you doing?

Say these sentences.
1. What were you **doing**?
2. What were you doing on **December 1**?
3. What were you doing on **Monday**?
4. What were **you** doing on your birthday?
5. What were **you** doing last winter vacation?
6. What were you doing **last night**?

Speechwork 10B

📻 **Listen and say.**
Is it **big** or **small**?   It's **small**.
Are they **dark** or **light**?   They're **light**.

Listen and say. Check (✓) the answer.
Is the shirt **striped** or **plaid**?   ☐ striped   ☐ plaid
Are the boots **big** or **small**?   ☐ big   ☐ small

👥 **Work with A.**

Listen to A's questions.
Answer A.

Ask A. Check (✓) A's answers.
1. Is the shirt **striped** or **solid**?   ☐ striped   ☐ solid
2. Is it **big** or **small**?   ☐ big   ☐ small
3. Are the sleeves **long** or **short**?   ☐ long   ☐ short

4. Is the sweater **checked** or **flowered**?   ☐ checked   ☐ flowered
5. Are the checks **gray** or **black**?   ☐ gray   ☐ black
6. Are the checks **light** or **dark**?   ☐ light   ☐ dark

Speechwork 11A

🔊 **Listen and say.**
The woman with the **red** hat isn't my mother.
The woman with the **green** hat is my mother.
The woman with the red hat isn't my **mother.**
The woman with the red hat is my **aunt**.

Listen and say. Circle the loudest word.
The man with the beard isn't my uncle.
The man with the beard isn't my uncle.

👤👤 **Work with B.**
Say these sentences.
1. The girl who's wearing glasses is my **cousin**.
2. The man with the **beard** is my uncle.
3. The boy in the **red** shirt is my nephew.
4. The boy in the red shirt is her **nephew**.
5. The woman with the hat is his **wife**.
6. The girl with the **dark** hair is his friend.

Circle the loudest words.
1. The man with the blond hair is her cousin.
2. The woman who is wearing the green dress is her friend.
3. The boy with the glasses is his son.
4. The man wearing the red shirt is his father.
5. The woman with the blond hair is her cousin.
6. The girl with the backpack is his niece.

Speechwork 12A

🔊 **Listen and say.**
He can **do** it.   She can **too**.
He **can't** do it.   She can't **either**.

Listen and say. Check (✓) your answer.
1. ☐ She can too.   ☐ She can't either.
2. ☐ He does too.   ☐ He doesn't either.
3. ☐ She should too.   ☐ She shouldn't either.

👤👤 **Work with B.**
Check (✓) your answers.
Say the sentences.
1. I ☐ can   ☐ can't   use a computer.
2. I ☐ can   ☐ can't   play tennis.
3. I ☐ can   ☐ can't   run fast.

Answer B. Say one of these.

I can.   I can't.
I can **too**.   I can't **either**.

Say these sentences.

1. She has a **bike**.
2. He **doesn't** have a **watch**.
3. She **shouldn't** watch TV so much.
4. I should **always** use English in class.
5. He **can't** run very fast.

Listen to B.
Check (✓) the right answer.
1. ☐ She does too.   ☐ She doesn't either.
2. ☐ He does too.   ☐ He doesn't either.
3. ☐ I should too.   ☐ I shouldn't either.
4. ☐ You should too.   ☐ You shouldn't either.
5. ☐ I can too.   ☐ I can't either.

Speechwork 11B

 Listen and say.
The woman with the **red** hat isn't my mother.
The woman with the **green** hat is my mother.
The woman with the red hat isn't my **mother**.
The woman with the red hat is my **aunt**.

Listen and say. Circle the loudest word.
The man with the beard isn't my uncle.
The man with the beard isn't my uncle.

Work with A.
Circle the loudest words.
1. The girl who's wearing glasses is my cousin.
2. The man with the beard is my uncle.
3. The boy in the red shirt is my nephew.
4. The boy in the red shirt is her nephew.
5. The woman with the hat is his wife.
6. The girl with the dark hair is his friend.

Say these sentences.
1. The man with the **blond** hair is her cousin.
2. The woman who is wearing the **green** dress is her friend.
3. The boy with the **glasses** is his son.
4. The man wearing the **red** shirt is his father.
5. The woman with the blond hair is her **cousin**.
6. The girl with the backpack is his **niece**.

Speechwork 12B

 Listen and say.
He can **do** it.   She can **too**.
He **can't** do it.   She can't **either**.

Listen and say. Check (✓) your answer.
1. ☐ She can too.   ☐ She can't either.
2. ☐ He does too.   ☐ He doesn't either.
3. ☐ She should too.   ☐ She shouldn't either.

Work with A.
Answer A. Say one of these.

I can.   I can't.
I can **too**. I can't **either**.

Check (✓) your answers.
Say the sentences.
1. I ☐ can ☐ can't speak English well.
2. I ☐ can ☐ can't type.
3. I ☐ can ☐ can't swim.

Listen to A.
Check (✓) the right answers.
1. ☐ He does too.   ☐ He doesn't either.
2. ☐ She does too.   ☐ She doesn't either.
3. ☐ I should too.   ☐ I shouldn't either.
4. ☐ I should too.   ☐ I shouldn't either.
5. ☐ She can too.   ☐ She can't either.

Say these sentences.
1. He **doesn't** have a **car**.
2. She has a **computer**.
3. I should **exercise** more.
4. You **shouldn't drive** so fast.
5. I **can't** understand **French**.

The numbers

1	2	3	4	5	6	7	8	9	10
one	two	three	four	five	six	seven	eight	nine	ten

11	12	13	14	15	16	17	18	19	20
eleven	twelve	thirteen	fourteen	fifteen	sixteen	seventeen	eighteen	nineteen	twenty

21	22	23	24	25	26	27	28	29	30
twenty-one	twenty-two	twenty-three	twenty-four	twenty-five	twenty-six	twenty-seven	twenty-eight	twenty-nine	thirty

40	50	60	70	80	90	100	1,000	10,000
forty	fifty	sixty	seventy	eighty	ninety	one hundred	one thousand	ten thousand

100,000	1,000,000
one hundred thousand	one million

The counting numbers

1st	2nd	3rd	4th	5th	6th	7th	8th	9th	10th
first	second	third	fourth	fifth	sixth	seventh	eighth	ninth	tenth

11th	12th	13th	14th	15th	16th	17th	18th	19th	20th
eleventh	twelfth	thirteenth	fourteenth	fifteenth	sixteenth	seventeenth	eighteenth	nineteenth	twentieth

21st	22nd	23rd	24th	25th	26th	27th	28th	29th	30th
twenty-first	twenty-second	twenty-third	twenty-fourth	twenty-fifth	twenty-sixth	twenty-seventh	twenty-eighth	twenty-ninth	thirtieth

31st	...100th	...1,000th	...10,000th
thirty-first	one-hundredth	one-thousandth	ten-thousandth

...100,000th	...1,000,000th
one hundred thousandth	one millionth